The Ultimate Unofficial Harry Potter® Trivia Book

The Ultimate Unofficial Harry Potter® Trivia Book

Secrets, Mysteries and Fun Facts
Including Half-Blood Prince
Book 6

Daniel Lawrence

iUniverse, Inc.
New York Lincoln Shanghai

The Ultimate Unofficial
Harry Potter® Trivia Book
Secrets, Mysteries and Fun Facts
Including Half-Blood Prince Book 6

Copyright © 2005 by Daniel Lawrence

iUniverse books may be ordered through booksellers or by contacting:

iUniverse
2021 Pine Lake Road, Suite 100
Lincoln, NE 68512
www.iuniverse.com
1-800-Authors (1-800-288-4677)

ISBN-13: 978-0-595-35500-6
ISBN-10: 0-595-35500-5

Printed in the United States of America

Copyrights, Trademarks, Etc.

Dedicated to
my wife, Lisa,
and my children,
Sara, Jenna and Joey
for their support,
encouragement and love.

CONTENTS

ACKNOWLEDGMENTS

I would also like to thank all of the numerous individuals who have helped make this book become a reality. First of all, I thank my publisher and my publishing associate, Rachel, for their assistance in writing this book. I can't thank you enough for being so helpful in its making. I'd also like to thank everyone in my family, including my wife, children and mother for allowing me the time to write and to attend to my various Potter engagements. Scott and Heather, thanks for your constant research and expert sleuthing.

I would like to thank J.K. Rowling for her inspirational writings and giving to all of us this beloved character and series. I would also like to thank the internet community and all the muggles worldwide who have always supported me and immersed themselves into the J.K. Rowling septology. Keep your love of reading. Develop your imaginations. Without you, Harry Potter would never be the wizard he is today.

INTRODUCTION

"*Harry Potter.*" Those two words evoke a range of emotions and images in almost anyone who hears them—and in most cases, a smile as well. His magical world brings together tens of millions of adults and children on a monumental reading fantasy, myself included. I still remember my first time reading a Harry Potter novel. I knew then how gifted a writer J.K. Rowling was and how brilliantly her words could transform you into her world. And I'm not alone. Harry Potter is the number one novel series in the world, with over 300 million copies sold worldwide.

It is somewhat hard to describe the special feeling I get when I'm immersed in a Harry Potter novel or film. Even if you've only read one book or seen just one film, then I think you know what I am talking about. From the moment you enter Harry's magical place, your own surroundings seem a million miles away. In other words, just as J.K. Rowling had hoped. You enter a world of mystery, magic and full of secrets. This mystical place is one of fantasy and adventure, where even adults can find an outlet and escape their troubles. The overall experience helps find the child in all of us. This is why Harry Potter is so loved.

The best thing about reading a Harry Potter book (HP) is the happiness you get from dissecting its contents and sharing the experience with other fans. Of course, there's a lot more to Harry Potter than you notice at first glance. The unparalleled attention to detail, to which fans tend to take for granted, requires a complex imagination that makes J.K. Rowling truly amazing. Few readers ever think about (and even fewer successfully figure out) the subplots and foreshadowing that occurs in each distinct book. Nor do a lot of fans recognize the incredible information and small touches sprinkled in dialogue and descriptions within each HP book that are placed simply to tease the readers who happen to notice them. Most readers don't realize that almost everything they read in Harry Potter has a purpose and a story behind it that gives it meaning.

About The Book

This book will assist you in discovering Harry Potter secrets, history, hidden meanings, and the little details that make these characters so beloved. It is divided into two parts. Part One covers the subject of Harry Potter in general. Part Two has a greater focuses on the author J.K. Rowling, the *Harry Potter and the Half-Blood Prince* book and the *Harry Potter and the Goblet of Fire* Movie. Each Part of this book begins with multiple-choice questions, followed by the correct answers and even some additional fun facts about the subject.

Harry Potter has gone through many changes in his six years at Hogwarts. So some questions let readers take a step back in time to revisit original character plots that have evolved over time. To add to the fun, you'll find fascinating tidbits of information highlighted throughout the book.

Looking for all the information you can get about a particular character, potion, place or whatever? Chances are it'll be in this book. However, don't be too disappointed if you don't find it. While this comprehensive book contains a multitude of questions about Harry Potter, the septology has thousands of details. One book simply cannot cover them all.

I certainly hope that you have as much fun reading this book as I did researching and writing it. I hope not only to enhance your love for Harry Potter, but to spark your interest in what makes the magic happen. Strangely enough, I find the more I learn about Harry Potter, the more magical this series becomes for me. I am still amazed at how each sentence or each new character taps my emotions and how I always finish a Potter novel with a smile on my face.

Spoiler Warning!

The Ultimate Unofficial Harry Potter Trivia Book is an ideal reference tool and companion piece for the Harry Potter Series and contains a comprehensive wealth of information. It is assumed that the reader has read the entire Harry Potter series of books.

Accuracy

All facts and statistics are accurate as of the time this book goes to press.

Did You Know?

Director Mike Newell only received $1 million to direct *Harry Potter and the Goblet of Fire* while Chris Columbus received $10 million plus a percentage of the gross when he directed *Harry Potter and the Sorcerer's Stone*.

PART ONE

1. What word coined by J.K. Rowling made it into the *Oxford English Dictionary*?
a.) Dementor
b.) Snape
c.) Gryffindor
d.) Muggle

2. How many voices did reader Jim Dale use in the audio version of *Goblet of Fire*?
a.) 102
b.) 114
c.) 127
d.) 149

3. How much is a signed first edition of the British version of *Harry Potter and the Sorcerer's Stone* worth (US$)?
a.) $15,000
b.) $18,000
c.) $23,000
d.) $39,000

4. What was the initial print run order for *Harry Potter and the Half-Blood Prince* book?

a.) 500,000

b.) 2.4 million

c.) 6.8 million

d.) 10.8 million

5. Which J.K. Rowling family member contends that he inspired the Harry Potter series?

a.) Brother-in-law Bob

b.) Uncle Phil

c.) Cousin Ben

d.) Nephew John

6. On the adult book cover of *Harry Potter and the Half-Blood Prince* (UK version), who is the author of "Advanced Potion Making"?

a.) Libatius Borage

b.) Libatius Bevora

c.) Libatia Bogata

d.) Liborium Borundum

7. What do the initials "J.K." stand for in J. K. Rowling?

a.) Jane Kathryn

b.) June Katelyn

c.) Joanne Kathleen

d.) John Koyle

8. In what year was the storyline for Harry Potter originally conceived by J. K. Rowling?

a.) 1988
b.) 1989
c.) 1990
d.) 1991

9. What mishap slowed the filming of *Harry Potter and the Prisoner of Azkaban*?

a.) tornado
b.) brush fire
c.) flood
d.) locusts

10. The game of Quidditch was invented in which century?

a.) 7th century
b.) 11th century
c.) 12th century
d.) 14th century

11. Which full scene did <u>NOT</u> make the final cut of the movie *Prisoner of Azkaban*?

a.) Sir Cadogan protecting Gryffindor Tower after Fat Lady is attacked
b.) Conversation where Mr. Weasley promises he won't look for Sirius
c.) Shrunken Head hangs from Knight Bus rear-view Mirror
d.) Malfoy draws caricuature of Harry

12. **What day is Nearly Headless Nick's deathday bash?**
a.) December 31st
b.) July 31st
c.) January 31st
d.) October 31st

13. **What was the first name of Hufflepuff's founder?**
a.) Hilda
b.) Helen
c.) Helga
d.) Huelwen

14. In Greek mythology, Hermione was the daughter of King Menelaus of Sparta and this famous beauty?
a.) Dido
b.) Aphrodite
c.) Helen of Troy
d.) Athena

15. What does Dumbledore say death is like to the well-organized mind?

a.) A trivia game

b.) The next great adventure

c.) The greatest spell

d.) A treasure of knowledge

16. What was used to nationally market the *Harry Potter and the Half-Blood Prince* book?

a.) Fleet of Blimps

b.) *New York Times* Crossword Puzzle

c.) Traveling Circus

d.) Computer virus

17. A card written by J.K. Rowling that contained 93 words about the *Harry Potter and the Order of the Phoenix* book was once auctioned for what sum?

a.) $34,918(US)

b.) $45,314(US)

c.) $51, 687(US)

d.) $79,102(US)

18. Which scene did the producers's unsuccessfully try to eliminate in the movie version of *Harry Potter and the Sorcerer's Stone*?

a.) Chocolate frog hopping out of Hogwarts Express

b.) Ron and Harry rescuing Hermione from the troll

c.) Harry unwrapping his Nimbus Two Thousand

d.) Seamus is accident-prone

19. What was the original name J. K. Rowling gave to Hermione?

a.) Palione

b.) Puckle

c.) Paisy

d.) Parione

20. On what television show did J.K. Rowling appear?

a.) *The Simpsons*

b.) *Spongebob Squarepants*

c.) *Friends*

d.) *Fear Factor*

21. Which character was to have a younger sister in the series?

a.) Dudley

b.) Snape

c.) Hermione

d.) Dumbledore

22. What Harry Potter based object was the subject of vandalism in 2001?

a.) Platform nine and three quarters

b.) Ford Anglia

c.) Muggle taxi

d.) Hogwarts Express Train

Did you Know?
Fortescue, the red-nosed Headmaster portrait in Dumbledore's office has the same name as Florean Fortescue, the owner of the ice cream shop located in Daigon Alley. Makes you wonder about a connection.

23. What quidditch position did James Potter play?
a.) Beater
b.) Keeper
c.) Chaser
d.) Seeker

24. Which wizard was clubbed to death in the Cotswolds while sketching?
a.) Emmeline Vance
b.) Millicent Bagnold
c.) Gondoline Oliphant
d.) Broderick Bode

25. Which of the following characters never called Voldemort by his proper name in books 1–5?
a.) Lupin
b.) Hermione
c.) Sirius
d.) Stebbins

26. How many points did Umbridge award Malfoy for catching Harry as he fled from the Room of Requirement?
a.) 10 points
b.) 20 points
c.) 50 points
d.) 60 points

27. Which character was developed but did not make the final draft of *Harry Potter and the Goblet of Fire* book?
a.) a cousin of Neville
b.) a sister of Cho Chang
c.) a cousin of the Weasleys
d.) a sister of Michael Corner

28. What house was the character Mafalda originally going to be placed in?
a.) Hufflepuff
b.) Gryffindor
c.) Slytherin
d.) Ravenclaw

29. The most dangerous beasts have what classification according to the Ministry of Magic?
a.) XXX
b.) XXXXX
c.) XXXXXX
d.) XXXXXXX

30. How many characters with new nationalities does author J.K. Rowling plan to introduce in Book 7 of the Series?

a.) One

b.) Two

c.) Three

d.) None

31. How much did Fred and George bet with Bagman during the Quidditch World Cup?

a.) 37 Galleons, 15 Sickles and 3 Knuts

b.) 37 Galleons, 13 Sickles and 5 Knuts

c.) 35 Galleons, 17 Sickles and 3 Knuts

d.) 35 Galleons, 15 Sickles and 7 Knuts

32. What type of Charm does Hermione place on the fake Galleons she gives the members of the D.A.?

a.) The Protean charm

b.) The Relashio charm

c.) The Tickling charm

d.) The Obliteration charm

33. In the film *Harry Potter and the Prisoner of Azkaban,* who threw a rock through the window of Hagrid's cottage that hit Harry in the head?

a.) Draco Malfoy

b.) Buckbeak

c.) Sirius Black

d.) Hermione Granger

> # Did You Know?
> If one person were to read every Harry Potter book ever sold-at a rate of one per day-it would take them over 700,000 years to do so.

34. Which of the following was partially converted to a Chinese Buffet?
a.) Martins Heron
b.) Shepperton Studios
c.) St. Pancras Station
d.) Nicolson's

35. How many fouls are recognized in the Department of Magical Games and Sports Records?
a.) 17
b.) 70
c.) 700
d.) 7,000

36. How any languages have Harry Potter books been translated into?
a.) 32
b.) 42
c.) 52
d.) 62

37. Which character broke the rules regarding visits to Hogsmeade?

a.) Dennis Creevey

b.) Roger Davis

c.) Cedric Diggory

d.) Marietta Edgecomb

38. Which country's World Cup performance led to it being included in the Quidditch World Cup?

a.) Ireland

b.) Britain

c.) Poland

d.) Bulgaria

39. How many people attended J.K. Rowling's October 2000 reading of excerpts from *Harry Potter and the Goblet of Fire* in Toronto?

a.) 2,000

b.) 8,000

c.) 20,000

d.) 35,000

40. Which job did J.K. Rowling perform prior to writing Harry Potter?

a.) accountant

b.) nurse

c.) engineer

d.) research assistant

41. What was the spell that Draco Malfoy used to make Harry's Legs move about?

a.) Severing Charm

b.) Tarantallegra

c.) Leg-Locker Curse

d.) Furnunculus

42. Which comedian was scheduled to play Peeves in the *Harry Potter and the Sorcerer's Stone* movie?

a.) Jay Leno

b.) David Letterman

c.) Ray Romano

d.) Rik Mayall

43. Professor McGonagall's first name, Minerva, is the Roman name for which Greek goddess?

a.) Artemis

b.) Athena

c.) Demeter

d.) Dido

44. Which wizard ate an entire Venomous Tentacula for a bet?

a.) Emeric the Evil

b.) Elfric the Eager

c.) Derwent Shimpling

d.) Uric the Oddball

Did You Know?

The death of Pope John Paul II caused his fifth and final book, *Memory and Identity*, to become the all-time bestseller in his native Poland. It eclipsed the previous record-holder *Harry Potter and the Order of the Phoenix*.

45. Which character is responsible to check daily for the births of any new magical children?

a.) Miles Bletchley

b.) Armando Dippet

c.) Professor McGonagall

d.) Cuthbert Mockridge

46. The International Confederation of Wizards first meeting was where?

a.) Poland

b.) Liechtenstein

c.) Germany

d.) France

47. What is the record for longest Quidditch match played at Hogwarts?

a.) Three Days

b.) Three Weeks

c.) Seven Weeks

d.) Three Months

48. What merchandise was NOT sold at the Quidditch World Cup?

a.) Bulgarian scarves

b.) Silk covered tasseled programs

c.) Model Firebolts

d.) Omnioculars

49. Three Galleons equals how many knuts?

a.) 87 Knuts

b.) 179 Knuts

c.) 1,479 Knuts

d.) 1,749 Knuts

50. How much would be the total cost to purchase three ounces of dragon livers and two bags of Knarl quills?

a.) 46 Sickles

b.) 63 Sickles

c.) 69 Sickles

d.) 73 Sickles

51. What best describes Pansy's dress robes?

a.) Shocking Pink

b.) Perfect Pink

c.) Frilly Pale Pink

d.) Fluffy Powder Pink

52. Which broomstick was used to fly to the Moon?

a.) Cleensweep Five

b.) Cleensweep Six

c.) Cleepsweep Seven

d.) Cleensweep Eleven

53. The Third Floor of St. Mungo's Hospital is used for treating?

a.) Broom Crashes

b.) Hexes

c.) Stings

d.) Regurgitation

54. Which of the following is <u>NOT</u> an Auror?

a.) Dawlish

b.) Arnie Peasegood

c.) Kingsley Shacklebolt

d.) Alastor Moody

55. Who refused to sign the International Ban on Duelling?

a.) Transylvanian Head of Magical Co-operation

b.) International Confederation of Wizards

c.) Dark Force Defense League

d.) Bulgarian Minister for Magic.

Did You Know?

To celebrate the release of the *Half-Blood Prince*, a Harry Potter conference in the UK was scheduled for July 2005 and includes "A Trial of Professor Snape" session in which the professor is brought up on charges to include his voluntary acceptance into the Death Eaters.

56. Which creature lives near Tibet and Nepal?
a.) Red Caps
b.) Nifflers
c.) Knarls
d.) Yeti

57. In the Spanish translation of Harry Potter, Trevor the Toad is said to be what?
a.) Turtle
b.) Tiger
c.) Owl
d.) Spider

58. Which Harry Potter character is <u>NOT</u> named after star formations in astronomy?
a.) Regulus
b.) Bellatrix
c.) Pucey
d.) Alphard

59. Which character is named after J.K. Rowling's grandfather?
a.) Seamus Finnigan
b.) Ernie Macmillan
c.) Anthony Goldstein
d.) Roger Davies

60. What primary factor forced the suspension in March 2005 of the *Harry Potter and the Goblet of Fire* filming for two weeks in Glencoe, Scotland?
a.) Labor strike
b.) Civil War
c.) Bad weather
d.) Copyright Infringement

61. The residents of what house are "just and loyal"?
a.) Hufflepuff
b.) Gryffindor
c.) Ravenclaw
d.) Slytherin

62. Which wizard is credited with founding a hospital?
a.) Mungro Bonham

b.) Mungro Bonheim

c.) Mungro Bollero

d.) Mungro Boudreis

63. How much (US$) did Scholastic Press pay for the initial American rights to the *Harry Potter and the Philosophers's Stone* book?

a.) $15,000

b.) $105,000

c.) $500,000

d.) $1 million

64. Who was Michael Corner's partner to the Yule Ball?

a.) Fleur Delacour

b.) Lavender Brown

c.) Parvati Patil

d.) Unknown

65. Which of the following is a head of Ravensclaw?

a.) Professor McGonagall

b.) Professor Sprout

c.) Professor Snape

d.) Professor Flitwick

66. What key ingredient does Harry forget to add to his Draught of Peace in Potions class?

a.) Two drops of syrup of Hellebore

b.) One pinch of Boomslang Skin

c.) An ounce of Armadillo Bile

d.) Powdered Bicorn Harn

Did You Know?

The movie *Harry Potter and the Goblet of Fire* running time is approximately 2 ½ hours in length. Thousands of fans unsuccessfully signed petitions to have the length extended to at least 3 ½ hours so that further details of the story could be more adequately represented.

67. What literary agency represents J.K. Rowling?
a.) John Foster
b.) Jose Cuerves
c.) Felix Schmidt
d.) Christopher Little

68. What was the name of the café where J.K. Rowling wrote *Harry Potter and the Philosopher's Stone?*
a.) Nearly's
b.) Nicolson's
c.) Nora's
d.) Nedbeck's

69. Who was the first witch to become Minister of Magic?
a.) Mafalda Hopkirk

b.) Williamson

c.) Millicent Bagnold

d.) Artemisia Lufkin

70. **Which monstrous eight-eyed spider, originally from Borneo, is capable of human speech and will try to eat any human that crosses its path?**

a.) Acromantula

b.) Gigantis Tarantula

c.) Manticore

d.) Borneaspula

71. **What name did J.K. Rowling originally give to Dean Thomas?**

a.) Dan

b.) Gary

c.) Craig

d.) Scott

72. **Which of the following was <u>NOT</u> discovered during the decontamination of Grimmauld Place?**

a.) Dead Puffskeins

b.) Rusty Scissors

c.) Coiled Snakeskin

d.) Order of Merlin Medal

73. **In the early draft of Book 1, which object did J.K. Rowling originally have appear in the Potters' vault in Gringotts?**

a.) Family Watch

b.) Small Dragon
c.) The Stone
d.) Diary

74. What are the names of Gilderoy Lockhart's two autobiographies?
a.) *Magical Me* and *How Do I?*
b.) *Magical Me* and *Who Am I?*
c.) *Magical Me* and *Just Be Me*
d.) *Magical Me* and *It's All Me*

75. Which of the following live in the lake on the grounds of Hogwarts?
a.) Grindylows
b.) Merpeople
c.) Giant Squid
d.) All of the above

76. What is the title of J.K. Rowling's favorite book as a child?
a.) *The Little Brown Horse*
b.) *The Little White Horse*
c.) *The Little Brown Cow*
d.) *The Little White Cow*

77. In Greek mythology, Hermione was the daughter of Helen of Troy and who?
a.) Zeus
b.) Hercules
c.) Prince Paris
d.) King Menelaus

78. Which charm is commonly used by witches being burned at the stake?
a.) Flame Freezing Charm
b.) Flagrate Charm
c.) Fidelius Charm
d.) Flipendo Charm

79. Which location was used to film the TriWizard Tournament in the movie *Harry Potter and the Goblet of Fire*?
a.) Black Rock Gorge

b.) Glen Navis
c.) Exmoor
d.) Ivinghoe Hills

80. What is J.K. Rowling's personal best at Expert Level Minesweeper?
a.) 101 seconds
b.) 99 seconds
c.) 94 seconds
d.) 91 seconds

81. What kind of weather did the bewitched windows at the Ministry of Magic display when the Magical Maintenance crew looked for a raise?
a.) 2 weeks of Tsunamis
b.) 2 weeks of Lightning
c.) 2 weeks of Hurricanes
d.) 2 weeks of Sleet

82. In the original game of Quidditch, besides watching the goalposts, what other duty did Keepers have?
a.) Yell at opposing players
b.) Try to snap the Golden Snitch
c.) Score goals with the Quaffle
d.) Provide refreshments

83. In the film *Harry Potter and the Prisoner of Azkaban*, what does Harry use to read under the covers at the beginning of the movie?
a.) Wand

b.) Flashlight

c.) Long Match

d.) Moonlight

84. J.K. Rowling was awarded her first honorary degree from which Ivy League school?

a.) Harvard

b.) Yale

c.) Princeton

d.) Dartmouth

85. Which spell is used to amplify ones voice?

a.) Siren Spell

b.) Serpensoria Spell

c.) Switching Spell

d.) Sonorus Spell

86. Actor Tom Felton, who plays Draco Malfoy, is known to have a problem with which of the following?

a.) Insomnia

b.) Stuttering

c.) Bulemia

d.) Reading

87. Paul Kieve served as an advisor during the filming of *Harry Potter and the Prisoner of Azkaban*. What is his area of expertise?

a.) Mythology

b.) Quidditch

c.) Illusion

d.) Labor relations

88. As further evidence that there are no limits to dissecting Harry Potter books, what question did fans at Reading University in the UK decide to study for a period in July of 2005?

a.) Whether Harry Potter is Male

b.) Whether Harry Potter is African

c.) Whether Harry Potter is Jewish

d.) Whether Harry Potter is Overweight

Did You Know?

If you wanted to be the first to see the new *Harry Potter and the Goblet of Fire* movie, you would need to fly to Belgium. It is released two days earlier than in the US and UK.

ANSWERS TO PART ONE

1. d.) *Muggle*
The word Muggle was included in the most recent update of the *Oxford English Dictionary*. Though J.K. Rowling coined it to signify a person with no magical powers, the OED says common usage has extended it to mean "a person who lacks a particular skill or skills, or who is regarded as inferior in some way."

2. c.) *127*
Jim Dale used 127 voices to read *Goblet of Fire*. He also recorded the audio version of *Harry Potter and the Order of the Phoenix*. The recording is 24 hours long.

3. d.) *$39,000*
A signed, first edition of *Harry Potter and the Philosopher's Stone*(UK), sells for upwards of $39,000. Only 600 copies of the UK first edition were printed.

Did You Know?

To commemorate her mother, J.K. Rowling donated a signed *Harry Potter and the Order of the Phoenix* book in April 2005 for auction to a charity in support of Multiple Sclerosis in Scotland.

4. d.) 10.8 million
The sixth in J.K. Rowling's blockbuster series, *Harry Potter and the Half-Blood Prince*, released to bookstores on July 16, 2005 had the all-time-highest initial print run of 10.8 million, which was four million more than for the *Harry Potter and the Order of the Phoenix* first run.

5. c.) Cousin Ben
J.K. Rowling's cousin Ben continues to insist that he inspired the Harry Potter book series. In a recent interview Ben was quoted as saying, "When I read the first Harry Potter book, my jaw dropped. It was uncanny, far more than a coincidence. I know Jo based Harry on me. I can see so much of the young me in his character." Ben even did a polygraph in 2005 to try to prove that he's the real Harry Potter on a TV show called *Lie Detector* on *PAX TV* in the US. On her official Web site *www.jkrowling.com*, J.K. Rowling has emphatically denied any truth to her cousin's claims.

6. a.) Libatius Borage
The UK adult version of *Harry Potter and the Half-Blood Prince* has a very old and battered copy of "Advanced Potion Making" on the book cover. It is from a photograph by Michael Wildsmith. Besides the UK, these covers appear on editions distributed in Britain, Canada, Australia, New Zealand, South Africa and many other countries throughout the world. The author of the book is Libatius means "libation" (liquid offering) in Latin, and Borage is a medical plant.

7. c.) Joanne Kathleen
Rowling thought that being a female may have hurt her chances of being published, so she began to just use her first two initials.

8. c.) 1990
J.K. Rowling stated on her official Web site that it was in 1990 that the idea for Harry Potter "simply fell into my head." Rowling and her then boyfriend had been in Manchester for a weekend of flat-hunting and the story of Harry Potter entered her mind as she was on a crowded train traveling back to London. However, it wasn't until six years later, in 1996, that J.K. Rowling received an offer from a publisher.

9. b.) *brush fire*
Sparks from the Hogwarts Express train started a fire during filming of *Harry Potter and the Prisoner of Azkaban* movie in Scotland, destroying nearly 80 acres of heather moorland.

10. b.) 11th Century
Quidditch dates back to the 11th Century.

11. a.) Sir Cadogan protecting Gryffindor Tower after Fat Lady is attacked
It was filmed but didn't make the final cut but look closely in the background when the Fast Lady tries to shatter a glass with the sound of her voice.

12. d.) October 31st
Nearly Headless Nick's deathday party is on October 31st, Halloween night.

13. c.) Helga
Hufflepuff's founder wanted to have Hogwarts include students from all backgrounds.

14. c.) Helen of Troy
When Helen sailed away with the Trojan prince Paris, she left behind nine-year-old Hermione, her only child.

15. b.) The next great adventure
Dumbledore's experience and his emphasis on knowledge led him to state his belief that death is but another adventure to those with a well-organized mind.

16. b.) Crossword Puzzle
A unique crossword puzzle entirely devoted to Harry Potter, which was a first time ever component of a children's book marketing campaign, was scheduled to run in *The New York Times* on Sunday, July 10th, 2005 to reach approximately 3.5 million readers. Also as part of the campaign, approximately 50,000 domestic flights on Continental Airlines and American Airlines were scheduled to feature 30-second and one-minute video ads.

17. b.) *$45,314*
A card which contained words central to the plot of *Harry Potter and the Order of the Phoenix*, was once auctioned for $45,314($US). The proceeds of the auction went to Book Aid International.

18. b.) Ron and Harry rescuing Hermione from the troll
J.K. Rowling diligently worked to keep this scene in the final version of the movie. Although the producers did not regard this scene as particularly important, Rowling believed that it was the cornerstone in developing the lasting friendship of characters Harry, Ron and Hermione. Of course, Rowling won and the scene was included in the final version of the movie.

19. b.) Puckle
On her official Web site, J.K. Rowling confirmed that Hermione's surname was to be Puckle, but she later modified the name to something she said would be less "frivilous", hence the character Hermione was born. Since Rowling knew many girls would identify with the Hermione character, she wanted an unusual name that had its own unique identity. Rowling also has stated that she considers Hermione to be an exaggerated version of herself when she was a young girl attending school.

20. a.) *The Simpsons*
In November of 2003, J.K. Rowling made a brief cameo on an episode of *The Simpsons*. In the episode, Rowling mentioned that after the Harry Potter series comes to an

end, Harry Potter would be fully grown and would then be ready to marry the show's character Lisa Simpson. Rowling was only joking!

21. c.) Hermione
J. K. Rowling stated that she originally wanted Hermione to have a sister in the series. Rowling apparently never found the right opportunity to introduce her fans to this new female character and subsequently abandoned the idea. JKR has indicated that with only book seven to complete, the storyline is currently too developed and too near the end to suddenly bring in a new sister for Hermione.

22. d.) Hogwarts Express Train
Two pieces of the train were covered in graffiti. The Hogwarts Express Train is commonly known as Loco No. 5972 Olton Hall and serves Scarborough and York in England by its operator, the West Coast Railway Company.

Did You Know?
In *Harry Potter and the Sorcerer's Stone* movie, a Chocolate Frog is seen hopping out of a window on the Hogwarts Express, yet in the book version, Chocolate Frogs are motionless.

23. c.) Chaser
J.K. Rowling recently stated in an interview with Scholastic books that although many fans believe he was a Seeker, James Potter was actually a Chaser.

24. c.) Gondoline Oliphant
According to her official Web site, J.K. Rowling indicates that this wizard (1720–1799) was famous for studies of life and habits of trolls.

25. d.) Stebbins
The dark character Voldemort has only been called by a handful of people in the Harry Potter books 1–5, including Lupin, Hermione and Sirius. Most characters will timidly only refer to Voldemort as You Know Who.

26. c.) 50 points
Harry also lost 50 points from Umbridge after learning of the interview in *The Quibbler*.

27. c.) a cousin of the Weasleys
A cousin of the Weasley was to have been in the *Harry Potter and the Goblet of Fire* book but was cut out of the final draft. J.K. Rowling spoke about the character during an April 2001 interview with BBC Newsround and indicated that she had created a female character named Mafalda. This character was to be the daughter of the Weasleys' accountant cousin who is a Muggle.

28. c.) Slytherin
J.K. Rowling had planned to place the non-existent Mafalda in the Slytherin house, thereby making this character a dark witch that most likely would have possessed many of the same talents as her cousin Hermione.

29. b.) XXXXX
The least dangerous beasts are classified as "X" while the most dangerous ones are "XXXXX".

30. d.) None
J.K. Rowling has already indicated in interviews that Hogwarts in a British institution and the book series is far too developed to bring in any new characters with new nationalities.

31. a.) 37 Galleons, 15 Sickles and 3 Knuts
The twins bet that Ireland would win the Cup.

32. a.) The Protean charm
Enables an object to change its form.

33. d.) Hermione
The scene of Hermione throwing the rock that hit Harry does not happen in the book version but was included in the movie.

34. d.) Nicolson's
Located in Scotland, the upstairs to this café in 2003 was sold and later reopened as a Chinese Buffet. This is the

place where J.K. Rowling did much of her initial writing on the Harry Potter series.

> ### Did You Know?
> Andorra is a small European community located between Spain and France. Its Minister of Magic was referenced in *Harry Potter and the Goblet of Fire*.

35. c.) 700
700 fouls are recognized by the Department of Magical Games. However, this list is not available for the wizarding public to access. The department feared that if players looked at the list, they might be tempted to perform some of these controversial moves.

36. d.) 62
Over 260 million copies in sixty-two languages have translated the works of Harry Potter.

37. a.) Dennis Creevey
According to the rules, only students who are at least in their third year are allowed to visit Hogsmeade. You may remember in your reading of the book that when he attended the Dark Arts meeting at the Hog's Head in Hogsmeade, Dennis Creevey was only in his second year.

38. d.) *Bulgaria*
J.K. Rowling was so impressed with its performance during the 1994 World Cup that she included this country in the Quidditch World Cup. Bulgaria surprisingly finished in fourth place during the 1994 World Cup.

39. c.) 20,000

40. d.) Research assistant
J.K. Rowling worked as a research engineer at Amnesty International. On her personal Web site, Rowling said that she found the job "interesting but I don't think I was much of an asset as I am terminally disorganized (see my desk top for a graphic demonstration)."

41. b.) Tarantellegra
This spell makes a person's legs dance uncontrollably.

42. d.) Rik Mayall
This English comedian was originally scheduled to play the role of Peeves in the *Harry Potter and the Sorcerer's Stone movie.* Unfortunately, Mr. Mayall didn't survive the final cut of the movie that was distributed worldwide.

43. b.) Athena
Athena was the Greek goddess of wisdom and the goddess of war and peace. She was a great help to heroes such as Odysseus and Hercules.

44. c.) Derwent Shimpling

According to her official Web site, J.K. Rowling indicates that Derwent Shimpling ate an entire Venomous Tentacula as part of a bet and he survived. Of course, he still remained purple.

Did You Know?

According to his official Web site, Daniel Radcliffe is a fan of the Fullham Football club and likes listening to music by such bands as "The Killers", "RazorLight", "The Pixies", and "The Sex Pistols." No mention of Elvis.

45. c.) *Professor McGonagall*

While being interviewed by Scholastic Books, J.K. Rowling indicated that Hogwarts has a magical quill that will write on parchment paper the names of any magical children born each day. Professor McGonagall has been assigned to review the names and he also sends owls to each magical child when they reach their eleventh birthday.

46. d.) France

Goblins were not permitted to attend the first International Confederation of Wizards and warlocks from Leichtenstein did not approve of Pierre Bonaacord as Supreme Mugwump.

47.) d. Three Months
According to Oliver, the longest Quidditch match was three months long. Talk about stamina!

48. b.) Silk covered tasseled programs
The merchandise sold at the Quidditch World Cup included velvet covered tasseled programs, not silk.

49. c.) 1,479 knuts
To do this problem, know there are 29 knuts to a Sickle and 17 Sickles to a Galleon. From this equation, we know that there are 493 knuts in one Galleon, so there would be 1,479 knuts in three Galleons.

50. b.) 63
Since readers are told in the series that dragon livers sell for 17 Sickles an ounce, three ounces of dragon livers would cost you a total of 51 Sickles. As one bag of Knarl quills cost six Sickles each, two bags would cost a total of 12 Sickles. Adding $51 + 12 = 63$ Sickles.

51. c.) Frilly Pale Pink
This color describes Pansy's dress robe.

52. b.) Cleensweep Six
According to *The Quibbler*, version number six was used by wizards to fly to the moon.

53. d.) Regurgitation
The third floor of St. Mungo's Hospital can treat rashes, uncontrollable giggling and regurgitation.

54. b.) Arnie Peasegood
Dawlish, Kingsley Shacklebolt and Alastor Moody are all Aurors, another name for dark wizard catchers. It is said that it takes over three years to become an Auror, and each must study such topics as Stealth and Tracking. Arnie Peasegood, by comparison, is an obliviator and casts memory charms on muggles that have viewed magic being executed.

55. a.) Transylvanian Head of Magical Co-operation
Many nations of wizards were strongly urged to execute the International Ban on Duelling Treaty. In addition, this province in Romania was mentioned by Lockhart as the place where he cured a Transylvanian of the Babbling Curse.

56. d.) Yeti
They live in the mountains around Tibet and Nepal and have thick white fur.

57. a.) Turtle
Trevor is a turtle in the Spanish translation.

58. c.) Pucey
Many characters such as Regulus, Sirius and Andromeda are named due to their connection with astronomy and constellations.

59. b.) Ernie Macmillan
Ernie MacMillan was the name of J.K. Rowling's grandfather. As a tribute to him, J.K. Rowling decided to include his name and assigned it to a character in the series.

60. c.) Bad weather
The Express newspaper in the UK reported during the filming in March of 2005 that "Warner Bros insiders have revealed that sets like Hagrid's House and Hogwarts School gatehouse in Glencoe will now be left unused after the cancellation of filming last week because of snow cost. A tented village for the stars was dismantled just seven hours after it was put up and helicopters were brought in to take away portable props off the hillside at Glenfinnan in the Highlands." One of the numerous possible site replacement for filming future Harry Potter films has even included the Czech Republic.

61. a.) Hufflepuff
With colors of black and yellow, Hufflepuff residents are just and loyal.

62. a.) Mungro Bonham

According to J.K. Rowlings official Web site, Mungro Bonham (1560–1659) was the famous wizard healer that founded St. Mungro's Hospital for the Magical Maladies and Injuries.

63. b.) $105,000 (US)

Scholastic Press bought the American rights to the book and paid the most ever given to a first work by an unknown author of children's stories.

64. d.) Unknown

At the traditional Triwizard Tournament Yule Ball held on Christmas Day, both Michael Corners and Dean Thomas took partners that are unknown.

65. d.) Professor Flitwick

Even though it has never ben stated in writing, J.K. Rowling did mention in an online chat with Barnes and Noble that Professor Flitwick is the head of Ravensclaw.

66. a.) Two drops of syrup of Hellebore

The Draught of Peace potion is normally used to soothe anxiety and agitation, however if not made exactly right, it can make the drinker enter a deep sleep.

Did You Know?
Shortly before the *Harry Potter and the Half-Blood Prince* book was released, UK publisher Bloomsbury redesigned its website to have the look of a spidery Aragog theme.

67. d.) Christopher Little
According to her Web site, the Christopher Little Literary Agency represents J K Rowling on a worldwide basis and with respect to all media—publishing, audio, film, TV and allied rights. Any queries with respect to rights, permissions, translations, interviews etc. in connection with J.K. Rowling or 'Harry Potter', should always be addressed to Christopher Little. The company also represents authors of both children's books and adult fiction and non-fiction works.

68. b.) Nicolson's
J.K. Rowling wrote *Harry Potter and the Philosopher's Stone* and many parts to the other books in this small café with her infant daughter in a stroller.

69. d.) Artemisia Lufkin

In her official Web site, J.K. Rowling indicated that Lufkin (1754–1825) was the first witch to become Minister for Magic.

70. a.) Acromantula

This monstrous eight-eyed spider, originally from Borneo, is capable of human speech and will try to eat any human that crosses its path.

71. b.) Gary

In her official Web site, J.K. Rowling originally gave the name of Gary to Dean Thomas. His storyline included his being raised by his Muggle mother and step-father. His biological father was a wizard and left the family when Dean was very young in order to protect them, but was murdered by Death Eaters. Dean was to have found out his family history during his stay at Hogwarts before J.K. Rowling decided to change the direction of Dean's character.

72. b.) Rusty Scissors

Although rusty daggers were found, no rusty scissors were ever mentioned during the time spent ridding the Place of Dark Ages objects and creatures so that it could be inhabited once more.

73. c.) The Stone

Rowling originally had the Stone appear in the Potters' vault. However, this would have changed the storyline in the first book (Did Lily and James steal the Stone from Flamel?) and she deleted it from the final print.

74. b.) *Magical Me* and *Who Am I?*
Magical Me and *Who Am I?*. Lockhart's autobiography, *Who Am I?*, was only shown in the *Harry Potter and the Chamber of Secrets* film.

75. d.) All of the above live in the Lake
(a) is correct because Grindylows attacked some of the champions during the second task of the Triwizard tournament. (b) is correct as it was described that the Merpeople live in an underwater village and speak Mermish. (c) is correct as giant squids regularly interact with students and are seen swimming in the water.

76. b.) *The Little White Horse*
This book, authored by Elizabeth Goudge, was a favorite of J.K. Rowling as she was growing up.

77. d.) King Menelaus
When Helen sailed away with the Trojan Prince Paris, Hermione was only nine years old and stayed with her father, King Menelaus of Sparta.

78. a.) Flame Freezing Charm
This charm is used to turn the fire's heat to a warm breeze, used by witches being burned at the stake.

79. b.) Glen Nevis

In September of 2004, Glen Navis was used to film the first task for the Triwizard Tournament. It is described as being the heart the Western Highlands, and having dramatic hills, green woodlands, heathermoors, and unforgettable views with magnificent sunsets.

80. b.) 99 seconds

On her official Web site, J. K,. Rowling proudly said that her personal best for Expert Level Minesweeper is ninety nine seconds. She states, "This goes to show how much time I have been spending at this computer, typing 'The Half-Blood Prince'. To those who suggest that I might get on even faster if I stopped taking Minesweeper breaks, I shall turn a deaf ear. It's either Minesweeper or smoking, I can't write if I have to give up both." Since this comment was first made, Book 6 has been published, so I'm sure she'll break her own record very shortly.

Did You Know?
Black Rock Gorge was used as a backdrop for one scene in the *Goblet of Fire* movie where Harry is chased into a gorge. It is a very deep and narrow 21,000-acre estate that is 125 feet (38 meters) deep, and one mile (1.6 Kilometers) long.

81. c.) 2 weeks of Hurricanes
Hurricanes were shown in the bewitched windows at the Ministry of Magic when the Magical Maintenance crew looked for a raise.

82. c.) Score goals with the Quaffle
In 1620 the rules were amended so that a Keeper only had to worry about guarding the posts.

83. b.) Flashlight
Harry reads using a flashlight to read his book at the beginning of film III. He reads using his wand only in the book. Isn't that just like Hollywood!

84. d.) Dartmouth
J.K. Rowling received her first honorary degree from this college in New Hampshire.

85. d.) Sonorus Spell
This spell is used to amplify a voice.

86. b.) Stuttering
Actor Tom Felton has speaking problems in private. His parents even had a doctor treating his stuttering during the filming of Harry Potter films. The problem is apparently not evident when he is in front of the camera.

87. c.) Illusion
The illusionist Paul Kieve served the film team as an adviser. He even taught some of the actors magic tricks

and made a brief appearance in the Hogsmeade pub "Three Broomsticks".

88. c.) Whether Harry Potter is Jewish

A presentation at Reading University is said to focus on the question of whether Harry Potter is Jewish. Reports that I have read have indicated that presenter Amy Miller believes the wizard created by JK Rowling has created "has a yiddishe neshama"—a Jewish soul. Another Reading program will additionally look into whether Harry Potter books are in any way connected to the Kabbala religion.

Did You Know?
Actor David Tenant who plays Barty Crouch Jr. in the *Harry Potter and Goblet of Fire* movie is also the tenth actor to play "Doctor Who" in the British television series.

PART TWO

1. Which historical event included a sub-committee of Sardinian sorcerers?
a.) Goblin Rebellions
b.) International Warlock Convention of 1289
c.) International Confederation of Wizards
d.) Warlocks Convention of 1709

2. How many types of Divination are practiced around the world?
a.) 6
b.) 16
c.) 60
d.) 160

3. How do you get into the Room of Requirement?
a.) Tickle the pear on the large portrait of a bowl of fruit on the fourth floor
b.) Walk seven times back and forth in front the Fat Lady while whistling
c.) Say "Oddsbodikans" while running up the Hufflepuff stairway

d.) Walk three times past the wall opposite the tapestry of Barabas the Barmy on the 7th floor, while thinking about what one needs

4. How many pages is the largest foreign Harry Potter hardcover edition book published to date?
a.) 2,212
b.) 2,600
c.) 3,200
d.) 4,200

5. Ladislaw Zamojski is the best Chaser on which National Quidditch team?
a.) Poland
b.) Britain
c.) Bulgaria
d.) Luxembourg

6. A Broomstick Servicing Kit contains which of the following?
a.) Gold Tail-Twig Clippers
b.) 24 Hour Emergency Card
c.) Sunglasses
d.) Brass Compass

7. The Hall of Prophecy is described as having what color candles?
a.) Violet-Colored
b.) Orange-shooting

c.) Blue-Flamed

d.) Red-glowing

8. Which book version of *Harry Potter and the Prisoner of Azkaban* contains the following paragraph?

"Harry's eyes snapped open. He was lying in the hospital wing. The Gryffindor Quidditch team, spattered with mud from head to foot, was gathered around his bed. Ron and Hermione were also there, looking as though they'd just climbed out of a swimming pool."

a.) US Version

b.) British Version

c.) Both Versions

d.) None

9. What zodiak sign is Harry Potter?

a.) Gemini

b.) Aries

c.) Leo

d.) Andromeda

Did You Know?

On its first day of sale in the UK, *Harry Potter and the Order of The Phoenix* sold at a rate of 21 books per second. If all those books sold in the UK in the first day were stacked up the pile would be 12 times higher than Mount Everest.

10. Which of the following did <u>NOT</u> happen to Neville in Book 4?

a.) Melted his seventh cauldron

b.) Got foot trapped in trick step

c.) Transplanted his ears onto a cactus

d.) Banished Flitwick instead of cushions across the classroom

11. In which year does a character Adrian not play a Slytherin Chaser?

a.) First year

b.) Second Year

c.) Third Year

d.) Fifth Year

12. Which bust is near the entrance to Gryffindor Tower?

a.) Boris the Bewildered

b.) Wilfred the Wistful

c.) Paracelsus

d.) Medieval Wizard

13. Which Magical Medicine cures boils?

a.) Calming Draught

b.) Phoenix Tears

c.) Pepperup Potions

d.) Murtlap Essence

14. Which of the following was <u>NOT</u> a prank done by Peeves?

a.) Played tennis in the Entrance Hall
b.) Threw water balloons
c.) Flooded the third floor
d.) Smashed cabinets

15. Which of the following is commonly associated with gypsies and the English?

a.) Patronus
b.) Tea Leaf Reading
c.) Star Charts
d.) Boggarts

16. Which of the following is a treatment for acne?

a.) Flutterby Bush
b.) Honking Daffodils
c.) Bubotubers
d.) Leaping Toadstools

17. In which book is a Dementor's Kiss <u>NOT</u> mentioned?

a.) Third
b.) Second
c.) Fourth
d.) Fifth

18. Where will you find Little Hangleton?

a.) 30 miles from the Isle of Wight
b.) 200 miles from Little Whinging

c.) 70 miles from Smeltings

d.) 12 miles from Hut-on-the-Rock

19. Before settling on Sorting Hat, J.K. Rowling originally envisioned the students to be sorted by what?

a.) Written exam

b.) Panel of ghosts

c.) Dice game

d.) Singing contest

20. Which of the following is a known alumni of Ravensclaw?

a.) Rabastan Lestrange

b.) Rosier

c.) Lasuris Bonao

d.) Fat Friar

21. Which of the following is a true definition of a hogshead?

a.) Formal clothing

b.) Imperial measurement

c.) Asian currency

d.) German auto

22. In the British edition of *Harry Potter and the Prisoner of Azkaban*, who is listed as the author of the book, *A History of Magic*?

a.) Wilbert Slinkhard

b.) Miranda Goshawk

c.) Bathilda Bagshot

d.) Adalbert Waffling

23. When is held the Second Task of the Triwizard Tournament?

a.) February 24, at half-past nine in the morning

b.) February 24, at dusk

c.) November 24 at half-past nine in the morning

d.) November 24 at midnight

24. Which of the following was <u>NOT</u> a precaution suggested by the Wizards Council to hide the existence of Quidditch from Muggles?

a.) Muggle-repelling charms should be used

b.) Game should be played at night

c.) The game should not be played within 100 miles of a town

d.) A tall wooden fence should be built around Quidditch pitches

Did You Know?

Worldwide money exchange company Travelex has an online Wizard-to-Muggle currency converter, that calculates the value of the dollar, pound, euro, rupee and other local monies into Galleons, Sickles, and Knuts.

25. What was the box office receipts total ($US) for the first Harry Potter film?
a.) 19 million
b.) 90 million
c.) 696 million
d.) 969 million

26. Which textbook can be used by Sixth years?
a.) *Ancient Runes Made Easy*
b.) *A Guide to Advanced Transfiguration*
c.) *Achievements in Charming*
d.) *Break with a Banshee*

27. In what year was the Glenfinnan Viaduct completed?
a.) 1894
b.) 1895
c.) 1896
d.) 1897

28. Which of the following is a Zonko Product?
a.) Butterbeer
b.) Belch powder
c.) Mulled Mead
d.) Pumpkin Fizz

29. In Book 3, in what month did Gryffinder play Ravenclaw?
a.) November
b.) May

c.) January

d.) February

30. In the film *Harry Potter and the Sorcerer's Stone*, the boa constrictor from the London Zoo is from where?

a.) Burma

b.) Buffalo

c.) Bolivia

d.) Bankok

31. Why is the sphinx classified as a beast?

a.) It only eats meat

b.) It was cannot speak to muggles

c.) It speaks only in puzzles and riddles and becomes violent when given the wrong answer

d.) It's claws are a serious danger

32. Who lives in Topsham?

a.) Professor Sprout

b.) Madam Z Nettles

c.) Lily Evans

d.) Molly Prewett

33. How many years were Ford Anglia's built in England?

a.) 9 years

b.) 15 years

c.) 21 years

d.) 27 years

34. The Original Order of the Phoenix were outnum-bered by Death Eaters?
a.) Five to One
b.) Ten to One
c.) Twenty to One
d.) Thirty to One

35. How many copies of *Harry Potter and the Order of the Phoenix* book sold in Britain in one day?
a.) 710,750
b.) 977,542
c.) 1,777,541
d.) 2,197,455

Did You Know?
The elaborately grotesque appearance of Mad Eye Moody in *Harry Potter and the Goblet of Fire* was created using prosthetic make-up rather than in post-production as the studios had originally requested.

36. In the *Harry Potter and the Prisoner of Azkaban* film, what are in Sirius Black's "Have you Seen This Wizard" Poster?
a.) 2 Runes
b.) 2 Constellations

c.) 2 Charms

d.) 2 Planets

37. How long is Fleur's wand?

a.) Nine and a half inches

b.) Ten and a quarter inches

c.) Eleven Inches

d.) Fourteen Inches

38. Which was <u>NOT</u> one of Dobby's Punishments?

a.) beat himself with a desk lamp

b.) Iron his fingers

c.) Beat his feet on the floor

d.) Hit himself with a flower pot

39. Which of the following is considered a Muggle Artifact?

a.) Ford Anglia

b.) Foe-Glass

c.) Hagrid's Umbrella

d.) Flying Carpets

40. Who many beds does the Knight Bus have?

a.) Six wooden beds

b.) Six brass beds

c.) Seven wooden beds

d.) Seven brass beds

41. What color uniform does Stan Shunpike have?

a.) Blue

b.) Green

c.) Magenta

d.) Purple

42. Which of the following was purchased for tax reasons?

a.) West Ham

b.) The Hanged Man

c.) Paddington Station

d.) Riddle House

43. How tall is the Post Office Tower?

a.) 610 feet

b.) 620 feet

c.) 670 feet

d.) 690 feet

44. Vauxhall Tube Station is located where?

a.) North end of London

b.) South end of London

c.) East end of London

d.) West end of London

45. What is the Capital City of Burkino Faso?

a.) Ouagadogou

b.) Ogagogana

c.) Odougadona

d.) Ougadoguaa

46. When is Hermione's Birthday?
a.) July 31
b.) October 31
c.) December 19
d.) September 19

47. In her second year, how long did it take Hermione to recover from transforming into a cat?
a.) Four weeks
b.) Five weeks
c.) Six weeks
d.) Seven weeks

48. Which of the following is <u>NOT</u> sold at Borgin and Burkes shop?
a.) Blood-strained playing card
b.) Glass eye
c.) Masks
d.) Canary Creams

49. What village did J.K. Rowling move to when she was nine years old?
a.) Tutshill
b.) Puddlemere
c.) Portree
d.) Chudley

Did You Know?
The city of Exeter in Britain had over 300,000 pre-orders for *Harry Potter and the Half-Blood Prince*, more than any other city in the UK.

50. What is the most favorite thing J.K. Rowling has bought with her earnings?
a.) House
b.) Automobile
c.) Yacht
d.) Helicopter

51. What Hogwarts house would J.K. Rowling be in?
a.) Gryffindor
b.) Hufflepuff
c.) Ravensclaw
d.) Slytherin

52. Which character does J.K. Rowling think is similar to herself in Quidditch ability?
a.) Harry
b.) Ron
c.) Hermione
d.) Neville

53. What occupation did J.K. Rowling's first husband have?

a.) animator

b.) book editor

c.) television journalist

d.) radio announcer

54. What subject did J.K. Rowling say she would like to teach at Hogwarts?

a.) Arithmancy

b.) Astronomy

c.) Divination

d.) Charms

55. For which charity did J.K. Rowling write *Fantastic Beasts & Where to Fund Them?*

a.) Tsunami Relief Fund

b.) Farm Aid

c.) Salvation Army

d.) Comic Relief

56. Which of the following gave J.K. Rowling her first publishing contract?

a.) Scholastic

b.) Penguin

c.) Bloomsbury

d.) Pendant

57. Which family member of J.K. Rowling has a scar similar to Harry Potter?

a.) Sister

b.) Uncle

c.) Cousin

d.) Aunt

58. Where did J. K. Rowling's father work?

a.) Scotland Yard

b.) *Virgin Airlines*

c.) *Hard Rock Café*

d.) *Rolls Royce*

59. What did J.K. Rowling buy for herself in 1997 when she won a grant from the Scottish Arts Council?

a.) Automobile

b.) House

c.) Computer

d.) Table

60. How many versions did J.K. Rowling write for the first chapter of *Harry Potter and the Philosopher's Stone*?

a.) One

b.) Five

c.) Ten

d.) Twenty

61. Who illustrated the US cover for *Harry Potter and the Half-Blood Prince* book?

a.) Mary O'Connor

b.) Mary Purdue
c.) Mary GrandPre
d.) Mary Duvet

62. How many pages is the deluxe version of *Harry Potter and the Half-Blood Prince*?
a.) 685
b.) 698
c.) 704
d.) 717

Did You Know?
In the movie *Harry Potter and the Goblet of Fire*, rather than using computer graphics, the film crew actually built a forty foot long dragon that could breath fire.

63. Which book in the series will be the longest?
a.) Book Two
b.) Book Five
c.) Book Six
d.) Book Seven

64. The cover of the US version of Book 6 is primarily green. Which of the following is <u>NOT </u>associated with the color green?
a.) Avada Kedavra

b.) Slytherin color

c.) Magic

d.) Doxycide

65. On the cover of Book 6, Harry holds his wand with his left hand. In which other book cover does he hold the wand in his left hand?

a.) Book Two

b.) Book Three

c.) Book Four

d.) Book Five

66. Academics from around the world are convening in Britain in late 2005 for the first Harry Potter conference. Which of the following will NOT be allowed to attend?

a.) Children

b.) Priests

c.) Americans

d.) Athletes

67. The opening chapter of *Harry Potter and the Half-Blood Prince* was originally to be used by J.K. Rowling in all the following books except?

a.) Sorcerer's Stone

b.) Prisoner of Azkaban

c.) Order of the Phoenix

d.) Goblet of Fire

68. What Award did Mr. Weasley win?

a.) Daily Prophet Grand Sickle Prize

b.) Daily Prophet Grand Prize Knut Award

c.) Daily Prophet Grand Prize Galleon Award

d.) Daily Prophet Grand Prize Wizarding Award

69. In *Harry Potter and the Half-Blood Prince* Book 6, which of the following is true?

a.) Harry stands another trial

b.) Luna and Neville Hook Up

c.) Dumbledore does not use the Harmonical Curse

d.) Harry has his longest stay ever on Privet Drive

70. When should Hermione's year-long ban on Rita Skeeter's writing have ended?

a.) end of May 1996

b.) end of June 1996

c.) end of July 1996

d.) end of August 1996

71. Which version of Book 6 contains the following passage:

"He looked rather like an old lion. There were streaks of grey in his mane of tawny hair and his bushy eyebrows; he had keen yellowish eyes behind a pair of wire-rimmed spectacles and a certain rangy, loping grace even though he walked with a slight limp."

a.) US Version

b.) UK Adult Version

c.) UK Children Version

d.) All

72. Which of the following characters makes an appearance in Book 6?

a.) Moaning Myrtle

b.) Tonks

c.) McClaggan

d.) All

73. When is Arithmancy taught to fifth years?

a.) Tuesday afternoons

b.) Nine o'clock in the morning

c.) Monday afternoons

d.) Wednesdays at midnight

74. Where did the Potters live according to J.K. Rowling's very first draft of the *Harry Potter and the Philosopher's Stone* book?

a.) Godric's Hollow

b.) Norfolk

c.) In a Subway Station

d.) On an Island

75. What words of advice did Dumbldore give during the second year?

a.) "Fear of a name increases fear of the thing itself."

b.) "Understanding is the first step to acceptance, and only with acceptance can there be recovery."

c.) "Indifference and neglect often do much more damage than outright dislike"

d.) "It is our choices that show what we truly are, far more than our abilities."

76. What town do the Weasleys live near?
a.) Ottery St. Catchpole
b.) Godric Hollow
c.) London
d.) Manchester

Did You Know?

J.K. Rowling lives on Earls Terrace in Kensington, west London, considered the most expensive street in England and Wales. If you want to be her neighbor, all you need is an average of $8,165,836.41(US) or £4,272,188(UK) to buy a house.

77. How fast can a Firebolt racing broom accelerate?
a.) 150 miles an hour in 10 seconds
b.) 150 miles an hour in 17 seconds
c.) 170 miles an hour in 10 seconds
d.) 170 miles an hour in 17 seconds

78. To where did Bertha Jorkins disappear?
a.) Bulgaria
b.) Poland
c.) Ireland
d.) Albania

79. What is the password to the Prefects' bathroom?

a.) Cockroach Cluster

b.) Lemon Sherbet

c.) Lemon Drop

d.) Pine-fresh

80. In Book 5, Umbridge put how many classes in detention for repeatedly fainting, bleeding and vomiting?

a.) 2

b.) 3

c.) 4

d.) 5

81. The rule that "teachers are forbidden from giving students any information unrelated to the subjects they teach" is commonly known as educational decree:

a.) Number Twenty-Four

b.) Number Twenty-Five

c.) Number Twenty-Six

d.) Number Twenty-Seven

82. Which of the following is <u>NOT</u> a chapter in Book 6?

a.) Draco's Mystery

b.) Spinners End

c.) Draco's Detour

d.) Felix Felicis

83. In *Harry Potter and the Half-Blood Prince* Book 6, which of the following is false?
a.) There is a new Minister of Magic
b.) Winky recovers from the Butterbeer addiction
c.) Draco and Hermione do not end up together
d.) Gawp becomes more agreeable to human contact

84. Where did James and Lily Potter get their money?
a.) Lottery
b.) Well-paid profession
c.) Inheritance
d.) Writing Books

85. Who is the sport Quidditch is named after?
a.) The person who invented it, Xavier Quidditch
b.) The Quidditch Plumbing Company that sponsored the early Quidditch teams
c.) The inventor of the sport lived near Queerditch Marsh
d.) The mascot of the first team was nicknamed Quidditch

86. During Harry's fifth year occlumency lessons, which of the following does Harry <u>NOT</u> see in Snape's memories?
a.) A girl laughing as he tries to mount a broomstick
b.) Being a teenager in his bedroom
c.) His parents arguing as he cries
d.) Dementors

87.) What did Elliot Smethwyck invent in 1820?

a.) Buckbeak saddle

b.) Cushioning Charm

c.) World's Fastest Broomstick

d.) New Quidditch point system

88. The Golden Snitch that the Seeker tries to capture is based on which of the following?

a.) Tiny fruit that ancient wizards used to eat

b.) A tiny bird that ancient wizards used to hunt

c.) A ball used in the ancient wizard sport of Golintheraus

d.) A picture that was traditionally placed on ancient wizard flags

89. Who is Deborah Purdue?

a.) Key character in Book 6

b.) Witch credited with starting the Gnome Revolution

c.) J.K. Rowling's midwife

d.) Quidditch world record-holder

90. What did UK Publisher Bloomsbury use for the printing of the UK version of *Harry Potter and the Half-Blood Prince*?

a.) 30% FSC Certified paper

b.) Animal blood mixed into the ink

c.) Children as proof readers

d.) Astrologers to select the initial release date

91. How many distinct classifications of Harry Potter cards are there?

a.) One

b.) Two

c.) Three

d.) Four

92. In *Harry Potter and the Half-Blood Prince* Book 6, which of the following is true?

a.) Rita Skeeter is ominously omitted

b.) Blaise Zabini is edited from the final version

c.) Professor Lockhart makes a guest appearance

d.) Petunia Dursley's character is further expanded

93. How will the Harry Potter series finally end in Book Seven?

a.) Harry lives, Voldemort dies

b.) Harry dies, Voldemort lives

c.) Both Harry and Voldemort live

d.) Both Harry and Voldemort die

Did You Know?

The *Harry Potter and the Goblet of Fire* video game has the players "feel the magic" as the controller shakes in reaction to the wand's motion. Also, there are modes that allow players to join forces to combine their skills and power.

ANSWERS TO PART TWO

1. b.) International Warlock Convention of 1289
Sardinian sorcerers formed a sub-committee at this convention.

2. c.) Over 160
Many kinds of divination are used around the world, including divination by sounds from the belly—Gastromacy, and divination by cheese—Tiromacy.

3. d.) Walk three times past the wall opposite the tapestry of Barabas the Barmy on the 7th floor, while thinking about what one needs.
After doing the ceremony, a polished door with a brass handle appears on the wall to gain access to the Room of Requirement. It is very difficult to find the room and many who do come across it by accident.

4. c.) 3,200
The largest British hardcover edition consists of 2,212 pages and the largest US edition has 2,689 pages. The largest foreign translation is to be a little over 3,200 pages in length.

5. a.) Polish National Team
Ladislaw Zamojski is this team's best Chaser.

6 d.) Brass Compass

A Broomstick Servicing Kit includes with a small brass compass, a silver (not gold) Tail-Twig Clippers, Handle Polish and a Do-it-Yourself Handbook.

7. c.) blue-flamed

The Hall of Prophecy is accessed by a door in the Time Room. It is a cold, cathedral-sized room lined with rows of dusty glass spheres on labeled shelves.

8. c.) Both

The passage appeared in Chapter 9 of both the US and British versions of *Harry Potter and the Prisoner of Azkaban*.

9. c.) Leo

As Harry was born on July 31, this makes him a Leo. So is J.K. Rowling.

10. a.) Melted his seventh cauldron

Although many things happened to Neville in Book 4, he only melted six cauldrons, not seven.

11. c.) Third Year

Adrian Pucey was a Chaser in Books One and Two and there was an Adrian mentioned as Chaser in Book 5. No character named Adrian was in Third year.

Did You Know?
In the movie *Harry Potter and the Goblet of Fire*, the body double for the Madame Maxime, the head of Beauxbatons, is played by a 7 foot 1 inch tall former athlete turned actor who also had previously worked on the *Predator* movies.

12. c.) Paracelsus
His bust is located on the seventh floor as is Lachlan the Lanky

13. d.) Murtlap Essence
This medicine was once used to soothe the pain in Harry's Hand and also cures boils.

14. c.) flooded the third floor
Peeves actually flooded the second floor, not the third floor.

15. b.) Tea Leaf Reading
This technique goes back hundreds of years and is associated with gypsies.

16. c.) Bubotubers
The giant black slugs have a yellow-green pus that smells like petrol but is great for acne.

17. b.) Second
In the Third Year, Fudge authorized a Kiss to be done on Sirius. In Book 4, while Fudge was questioning a suspect, a Dementor kissed the suspect. In Book 5, a Muggle was kissed by two Dementors that appeared in an alleyway. Book 2 does not mention a Dementor's Kiss.

18. b.) 200 miles from Little Whinging
This is the location of Little Hagleton. Please note that in Southern England in Sussex County there actually is a Hangleton.

19 b.) Panel of ghosts
J.K. Rowling originally thought of having the students being sorted by a panel of ghosts that passed through a magical gateway as names were drawn out of a hat.

20. c.) Lasuris Bonao
He is one of the only known alumni of Ravensclaw.

21. b.). Imperial measurement
A Hogshead is actually defined as being an old imperial measurement that is the equivalent of 14,653 cubic inches or two liquid barrels.

22. d.) Adalbert Waffling is the UK author.
Bathilda Bagshot is the named author in the American edition of the book. Wilbert Slinkhard wrote *Defensive Magical Theory* and Miranda Goshawk write *The Standard Book of Spells, Grade 4.*

23. a.) February 24, at half-past nine in the morning
This is when the second task is held.

24. d.) A tall wooden fence should be built around Quidditch pitches

25. d.) 969 million
Makes it the third most successful film of all-time.

26. b.) A Guide to Advanced Transfiguration
The first time we read about this textbook is during Harry's fourth year when Cedric, two years older than Harry used it.

27. a.) 1894
This historic structure can be seen in the Harry Potter movies carrying the Hogwarts Express. The viaduct is 1,248 feet long and crosses over the River Finnan Valley. It also has 21 arches and is 100 feet high.

28. b.) Belch Powder
This Zonko Product is a favorite of George and Fred Weasley.

29. d.) February
The final score was 230 to 30 for Gryffindor.

Did You Know?
The total number of Harry Potter books ever sold is more than the populations of Britain, France, Germany and Italy combined!

30. a.) Burma
In the book version, the boa constrictor from the Zoo is from Brazil.

31. c.) It speaks only in puzzles and riddles and becomes violent when given the wrong answer.
A sphinx is classified as a beast.

32. b.) Madam Z Nettles
This qwikspell student lives in Topsham which is part of Exeter, in Devon.

33. a.) 9 years
Over one million of these cars were produced from 1959 until 1968.

34. c.) Twenty to One
Lupin indicated that when the Order of the Phoenix group began in 1970's, it was 20 to 1.

35. c.) 1,777,541
In Britain, this amount of book sales made Book 5 the fasting selling book of its time.

36. a.) 2 Runes
They are "perth", which looks like a sideways tophat and "algiz" which looks like a Y with an extra line up the middle. Perth is defined as secret or hidden things, whereas Algiz means protection or advisor.

37. a.) Nine and a half inches
Fleur's wand includes rosewood and Veela hair.

38. d.) Hit himself with a flower pot
Dobby hit himself with a water jug, not a flower pot. He believes in self-punishment when he breaks certain rules. Among his punishments have been pinching his ears and bang his head against a wooden table.

39. d.) Flying Carpets
They are on the Registry of Proscribed Charmable Objects and have been under embargo. Crouch's grandfather had one that could seat up to 12 before these carpets were banned.

40. b.) Six brass beds
On the ground level are the beds, which become chairs during the day.

41. d.) Purple
Stan also has some big ears! Stan is the bus conductor and is only a few years older than Harry. He has even bragged to Veela that he will become the youngest ever Minister of Magic.

42. d.) Riddle House
It is located on top of a hill. Over time, the house became vacant and children of the village were said to vandalize is quite often. Eventually a wealthy man bought the house for tax matters, but he didn't actually move into it.

43. b.) 620 feet
When it opened in 1965 the Post Office Tower was the tallest in England

44. b.) South end of London
Tom Riddle bought his diary in Vauxhall Road.

45. a.) Ouagadogou
Burkina Faso is a small African nation where Lockhart once claimed that he saved the townspeople by giving them amulets.

46. d.) September 19
Hermione was born in September and Fred and George were born on April Fool's Day.

47. b.) Five weeks.

In her stay at the hospital wing, Hermione's recovery time was about five weeks after she accidentally transformed into a cat. You may remember that during her stay she kept a card she received from Lockhart under her pillow.

Did You Know?
If all the Harry Potter books ever sold were laid flat, they would cover the area of about 1000 football pitches. Or they could be used to carpet Monaco 3.7 times.

48. d.) Canary Creams

Blood-stained playing cards, glass eyes and Masks are all items that are sold at Borgin and Burkes, the largest shop in Knockturn Alley. Canary Cream is not a product said to be sold at this shop, however it is one of the products that is sold at Weasleys' Wizard Wheezes along with such items as Extendable ears and Skiving snackboxes.

49. a.) Tutshill

This village is located in southern England, in the county of Gloucestershire. The Quidditch team, the Tutshill Tornadoes, bears the similar name.

50. a.) House
J.K. Rowling stated that "My favorite material thing is our house in the north of Scotland, where it is very peaceful and we have a lot of fun with family and friends. Probably the very best thing my earnings have given me, though, is absence of worry. I have not forgotten what it feels like to worry whether you'll have enough money to pay the bills. Not to have to think about that any more is the biggest luxury in the world."

51. a.). Gryffindor
Rowling has made it known many times that she values courage above anything.

52. d.) Neville
J.K. Rowling once remarked in an online chat for World Book Day in 2004 that "I'm not sporty, I'm not great with heights, and I'm clumsy as well—Neville's flying ability would be about my standard."

53. c.) Television journalist
J.K. Rowling married Portuguese television journalist Jorge Arantes in 1992 but later divorced him.

54. d.) Charms
J.K. Rowling said she would like to teach charms if she was ever a teacher at Hogwarts.

55. d.) Comic Relief
J.K. Rowling wrote this book in 2001 as a fundraiser for the UK charity Comic Relief that helps children in some of the poorest countries.

56. b.) Bloomsbury
It took over one year for J.K. Rowling's agent to find a publisher willing to take a chance on *Harry Potter and the Philosopher's Stone*. In August of 1996, J.K. Rowling received an advance from Bloomsbury.

57. a.) Sister
Rowling's sister Di has a scar similar to Harry Potter.

58. d.) *Rolls Royce*
Rowling's father worked on airplane engines for Rolls Royce

59. c.) Computer
Rowling bought herself a computer in 1997 after she won a grant from the Scottish Arts Council. She can afford a few of them now!

60. c.) Ten
She wrote ten versions of the first chapter of *Harry Potter and the Philosopher's Stone*.

61. c.) Mary GrandPre
The cover of "*Harry Potter and the Half-Blood Prince*" depicts a 16-year-old Harry looking very attentive and

Dumbledore with his hand extended as they look into a basin from which a mysterious green light is emanating."In creating the Harry Potter artwork, I try to bring a certain amount of realism and believability to the characters and setting, but still add an element of wonder and the unknown," said Mary GrandPre on the *Today Show* on NBC TV. "For the cover of *Harry Potter and the Half-Blood Prince*, the mood of the art is truly eerie. I wanted the colors to be strong and I chose upward lighting and dramatic shadows to convey a kind of surreal place and time. It is an honor to illustrate for such an amazing writer as J.K. Rowling. She gives me, as an illustrator, so much to work with."

Did You Know?
Hagrid's Hut in the movie version is made of stone while it is described as being a wooden shack in the books.

62. c.) 704
Scholastic Books decided to release of a deluxe edition of *Harry Potter and the Half-Blood Prince*. This edition includes a 32-page insert on special paper at the end of the book featuring near scale reproductions of Mary GrandPre's interior art, as well as a never-before-seen piece of full-color-art for the frontpiece. The book, which comes in a foil-stamped cardboard slipcase

printed with the *Harry Potter and the Half-Blood Prince* cover image, also includes a blind-stamped cloth case, full-color endpapers printed with the jacket art from the regular edition, luxurious foil, and a wraparound jacket featuring exclusive, suitable-for-framing art from Mary GrandPre. The deluxe edition has a total of 704 pages.

63. d.) Book Seven

When asked, J.K. Rowling has already stated in inteviews that the final book in the series would be the longest, as she dreads having to finish writing the series, and will probably just keep "writing and writing" it.

64. b.) Doxycide

The color of the mist on the book cover is green, a color associated with magic and also to the Slytherin colors of green. It is also associated with the killing curse Avada Kedavra. Doxycide is a noxious black liquid.

65. d.) Book Five

In Book One, Harry said his wand arm was his right hand. However, in Books Five and Six Harry holds his wand in his left hand.

66. a.) Children

Academics from around the world convene in Britain for the first Harry Potter conference in July of 2005 and is open to the public. There was to be staged a mock trial of Snape, the potions master at Hogwarts' School of Witchcraft and Wizardry. In spite of the fact that Harry

Potter books are aimed mainly at children, those under eighteen years of age are banned from the conference because of its academic content and more importantly; because there will be a bar!

67. d.) Goblet of Fire

68. c.) Daily Prophet Grand Prize Galleon Award
Mr. Weasley won the award and took the family to Egypt.

69. c.) Dumbledore does not use the Harmonical Curse
Rowling does not see Luna and Neville finding true love in Books 6 or 7. In an interview conducted before the release of Book Six, Rowling was quoted as saying "The Luna/Neville shippers are much less vehement and scary than the Harry/Hermione, Ron/Hermione tribes, so I hope I won't receive too much hate mail for quashing this rumour. I see Neville and Luna as very different kinds of people and while they share a certain isolation within Hogwarts, I don't think that's enough to foster true love—friendship, perhaps, although I think that Neville would always find Luna's wilder flights of fancy alarming."

As for Harry, Rowling does not have Harry stand another trial in Book Six and he has his shortest time ever on Privet Drive. Rowling indicated that "The next book, Half Blood Prince, is the least that you see of the Dursleys. You see them quite briefly. You see them a bit more in the final book, but you don't get a lot of Dudley in book six very few lines. I am sorry if there are Dudley fans out there, but I think you need to look at your priorities if it is Dudley that you are looking forward to."

70. b.) end of June 1996
Barring an unexplained incident, Hermione's one year ban will end in June of 1996

71. d.) All
The US, UK Adult and Childrens all have the passage.

72. d.) All
At the Edinburgh Book Festival, Rowling was quoted as saying "there is a McClaggan in book six because I thought that it is a surname that is too good to waste."

73. c.) Monday afternoons
This form of numerology based on Ancient Greek and Chaldean methods is taught to both fourth and fifth years on Monday afternoons. Third years have it at 9 o'clock in the morning.

74. d.) On an Island
On her official website, J.K. Rowling said "There were many different versions of the first chapter of *'Philosopher's Stone'* and the one I finally settled on is not the most popular thing I've ever written; lots of people have told me that they found it hard work compared with the rest of the book. The trouble with that chapter was (as so often in a Harry Potter book) I had to give a lot of information yet conceal even more. There were

various versions of scenes in which you actually saw Voldemort entering Godric's Hollow and killing the Potters and in early drafts of these, a Muggle betrayed their whereabouts. As the story evolved, however, and Pettigrew became the traitor, this horrible Muggle vanished.

Other drafts included a character by the name of 'Pyrites', whose name means 'fool's gold'. He was a servant of Voldemort's and was meeting Sirius in front of the Potters' house. Pyrites, too, had to be discarded, though I quite liked him as a character; he was a dandy and wore white silk gloves, which I thought I might stain artistically with blood from time to time.

The very, very earliest drafts of the first chapter of 'Philosopher's Stone' have the Potters living on a remote island, Hermione's family living on the mainland, her father spotting something that resembles an explosion out at sea and sailing out in a storm to find their bodies in the ruins of their house. I can't remember now why I thought this was a good idea, but I clearly recognised that it wasn't fairly early on, because the Potters were relocated to Godric's Hollow for all subsequent drafts."

Did You Know?
For the movie *Harry Potter and the Goblet of Fire*, a 30-foot maze that is featured in the tri-wizard tournament was actually built at Pinewood Studios before it was replicated in the Scottish valley where Hogwarts is situated.

75. d.)
Dumbledore offers many pieces of mysterious advice in all the books. In book 2 of the series, Dumbledore gave his all-knowing "It is our choices that show what we truly are, far more than our abilities."

76. a.) Ottery St. Catchpole
Besides the Weasleys, also the Diggorys, Lovegoods and Fawcetts all live in the area of Ottery St. Catchpole.

77. a.) 150 miles an hour in 10 seconds
Pretty fast for a broom, don't you think? You better ask the price before you buy one.

78. d.) Albania
Watch out for Bertha Jorkins the next time you're in Albania.

79. d.) Pine-fresh
Opens the Prefects bathroom.

80. c.) 4
Umbridge put a total of 4 classes in detention after failing to discover why students were constantly fainting and vomiting.

81. c.) Number Twenty-Six
The Ministry gave the Hogwarts High Inquisitor complete authority to implement new rules that related to education at Hogwarts. Number Twenty-Six dealt with limiting teachers to give information on unrelated topics. Afterward, Number Twenty-Seven was enacted that served notice to any student that they would be expelled if caught with a copy of *The Quibbler.*

82. a.) Draco's Mystery
Draco's Detour is the correctly named chapter in *Half-Blood Prince.*

83. b.) Winky recovers from Butterbeer addiction
In Book 6, Rowling decided to make a new Minister of Magic, After much debate, when asked about the possibility of a new minister of Magic, Rowling stated in her World Book Day Chat "Yes. Ha! Finally, a concrete bit of information, I hear you cry!"
As for Gawp, J.K. Rowling gave insight by saying "Grawp is obviously the very stupidest thing that Hagrid ever

brought home. In his long line of bringing home stupid things÷Aragog, the Blast-Ended Skrewts÷Grawp is the one that should have finished him off, but ironically it might be the one time that a monstrous something came good. By the next book, Grawp is a little bit more controllable. I think you got a clue to that at the end of Phoenix, because Grawp was starting to speak and to be a little bit more amenable to human contact."

Finally, Rowling has stated in interviews that Hermione and Draco "Will they end up together in book six/seven? NO! The trouble is, of course, that girls fancy Tom Felton, but Draco is NOT Tom Felton!" But Rowling has stated that Winky never will recover from addiction to Butterbeer.

84. c.) Inheritance

J.K. Rowling has indicated that James inherited plenty of money, so he didn't need a well-paid profession. You'll discover even more about both of Harry's parents in Book 7.

85. c.) The inventor of the sport lived near Queerditch Marsh

86. d.) Dementors

Snape saw Dementors in Harry's dreams and memories. However, Harry never saw them when he analyzed Snape's memories.

87. b.) Cushioning Charm
It was invented to make playing Quidditch more comfortable.

88. b.) Tiny bird that wizards used to hunt
Capturing a tiny bird called a Golden Snidget was originally part of the sport of Quidditch. However, this bird soon became an endangered species. A brilliant wizard by the name of Bowman Wright created a metal substitute which he bewitched so it would fly around the Quidditch field, resembling the bird.

Did You Know?

After filming is completed for *Harry Potter and the Order of the Phoenix,* director David Yates wants to do a movie version about a 1950's comedian named Frank Randle.

89. c.) J.K. Rowling's midwife
J.K. Rowling had three children. Jessica, David and Mackenzie. Just like the birth of her son David, the birth of Mackenzie in 2005 was attended to by a private midwife named Deborah Purdue. Although she no longer lives in Scotland, Ms. Purdue made regular visits to the Rowling household.

90. a.) 30% Forest Stewardship Council (FSC) certified paper

In a March 5, 2005 article on *Greenbiz.com*, J.K. Rowling's publisher Bloomsbury indicated that *"Harry Potter and the Half Blood Prince* would be printed on 30% Forest Stewardship Council (FSC) certified paper. This will make it the first best-selling book in the U.K. to be printed on such paper stock. According to environmental nonprofit Greenpeace, Bloomsbury has positioned itself as the most environmentally progressive of the major U.K. publishers to date. Other publishers, including Random House and Harper Collins, have so far failed to respond. Greenpeace is campaigning to get the book industry to stop sourcing paper from ancient forest regions and move towards using 100% ancient forest friendly paper. According to environmental nonprofit Greenpeace, Bloomsbury has positioned itself as the most environmentally progressive of the major U.K. publishers to date. Other publishers, including Random House and Harper Collins, have so far failed to respond. Greenpeace is campaigning to get the book industry to stop sourcing paper from ancient forest regions and move towards using 100% ancient forest friendly paper. She continued, "We welcome the efforts that Bloomsbury have made and look forward to them moving towards 100% ancient forest friendly papers for all future Harry Potter print runs and their other titles."

In the summer of 2004, Bloomsbury made an initial step towards going ancient forest friendly by printing the children's and adult's versions of the paperback of *Harry*

Potter and the Order of the Phoenix on 10% and 20% recycled paper respectively, measures obviously approved by J.K. Rowling.

91. c.) Three
I am asked this question frequently and there are primarily three types of Harry Potter cards. The first is the Harry Potter Trading Card Game, which Wizards of the Coast started distributing several years ago. The second type of Harry Potter cards were trading cards with photos from the films. These cards offer no additional information and are simply souvenirs of the films. The third type of cards are the Famous Wizard cards. These cards can be found in several forms to include the candy Chocolate Frogs you can buy in stores. They also appear in the Electronic Arts video games, and it is from these games that you can get the entire list of cards.

92. d.) Petunia Dursley's character is further expanded
J.K. Rowling told fans as far back as 2004 about Petunia Dursley and the fact that there was more to her than what appeared on the surface to her limited character in Books One to Five. Finally, Book 6 was where J.K. Rowling found it appropriate to delightfully expound the Petunia character for us.

93. ??
Although you might think I already know the answer, only J.K. Rowling herself knows for certain how Book 7

will eventually end. Still, it sure is fun being a sleuth and trying to figure it all out!

> ### Did You Know?
> **J.K. Rowling thinks *Harry Potter and the Half-Blood Prince* may be her favorite book in the series. But then again, she hasn't completed writing Book Seven as of yet!**

AUTHOR'S NOTE

As said in the Introduction, while this book contains numerous trivia questions, the Harry Potter story has thousands of nooks and crannies and the series is constantly evolving. No one book will ever cover it all. But that's good news for trivia lovers; there'll always be something new to look forward to. I again wish to acknowledge all my associates, friends and muggle fans around the world for your support. Thank you for believing. Enjoy and remember that the countdown to Book Seven is never too early to begin!

BIBLIOGRAPHY

The following Web sites are recommended and contain highly accurate information on Harry Potter:

WEB SITES

Bloomsbury.com
DarkMark.com
Godrics-hollow.net
Harrypotterfanzone.com
HPANA.com
J.K. Rowling.com
The-leaky-cauldron.com
Mugglenet.com
Scholastic.com
Thesnitch.co.uk
Wizardnews.com

BOOKS

Some of the information in *The Ultimate Unofficial Harry Potter Trivia Book* came from the following sources:

"Animal Guides," PathWalkers.net.

Online.www.pathwalkers.net/animalguides/index.html

"Animal Symbolism," *Princeton Online.*

Online.Www.princetonon/com/groups/iad/Files/animals.htm

Association of British Counties. Online.www.abcounties.co.uk

Astro Chat with June. Online.astrochat-with-june.com/signs.htm

"Australia House," *Australia High Commission UK.*

Online.www.australia.org.uk

Behind the Name. Online.www.babynamenetwork.com

"Black Park" *Visit Buckinghamshire.*

Online.www.visitbuckinghamshire.org

Boyle, Fionna, *A Muggles Guide to the Wizarding World.* ECW Press.
2004

British Tourist Authority. Online.www.visitbritain.com

Burdick Harmon, Melissa. "J.K. Rowling: The Real-Life Wizadr
Behind Harry Potter,"*Biography*, September 2003

Carter, Larry. Pagan Magick & The Rowan Tree," *Rowan.*

Online.www.angelfire.com/ks/larrycarter/Rowan/Tree.html

Celtic Tree Lore. Online.www.dutchie.org/Tracy/tree.html

"The Constellations," *CosmoBrain Astronomy and Astrophyics.*

Online.www.cosmobrain.com

DarkMark. Online.www.darkmark.com

Dragons of the British Isles.

Online.www.wyrm.org.uk/ukdracs/indesx.html

"Dream Dictionary," *DreamMoods.* Online.www.dreammoods.com

Early British Kingdoms. Online.www.earlybritishkingdoms.com

Encyclopedia Mythica. Online.www.panteon.org

Factmonster.com

Fictional cash fools Potter fans," *BBC News.* Online.news.bbc.co.uk.
April 2004

"Fort William and Area," *Intenet Guide to Scotland.*

Online.www.scotland-inveness.co.uk/fortwill.htm

Fraser, Lindsay. "Harry Potter—Harry and me," *The Scotsman.*

news.scotsman.com/.November 2002

Freesearch Bristish English Dictionary.
Online.www.freesearch.co.uk/dictionary
Godrics Hollw. Online.www.godrics-hollow.net
Gods, Heroes and Myth. Online.www.gods-hereos-myth.com
Harry Potter and the Chamber of Secrets," *Internet Movie Database*.
Online.www.imbd.com/title/tt0295297/
Harry Potter and the Chamber of Secrets," *Movie Mistakes*.
Online.www.moviemistakes.com/film2434
"Harry Potter and the Philosopher's Stone," *Movie Mistakes*.
Online.Online.www.moviemistakes.com/film1654
"Harry Potter and the Philosopher's Stone," *The Worldwide Guide to Movie Locations*. Online.www.movie-locatioons.com/movies/h/harry_potter1.htm
"Harry Potter Books from Bloomsbury," *Bloomsbury.com*.
Online.www.bloomsbury.com/harrypotter/muggles_index.html
"Harry Potter from Glencoe," *Glencoe Scotland*.
Online.www.glencoescotland.com
Harry Potter Lexicon. Online.www.hp-lexicon.org.
Harry Potter News Review More.
Online.www.kewlplaces.net/moviesnews
Hartland, Edwin Sidney. "English Faerie and other Folk Tales," *Internet Sacred Text Achive*.
Online.www.sacred-texts.com/neu/eng/efft
HPANA (Harry Potter Automatic News Aggregator).
Online.www.hpana.com
J.K. Rowling. Online.www.jkrowling.com
"J.K. Rowling's Notebook," *The Crusaders*.
Online.www.crusaders.no/-afhp/notebook
Kloves, Steven (writer) and Columbus, Christopher (director). *Harry Potter and the Sorcerer's Stone*. Motion Picture. Warner Brothers. November 2001
Kloves, Steven (writer) and Columbus, Christopher (director). *Harry Potter and the Chamber of Secrets*. Motion picture. Warner Brothers. November 2002

Kloves, Steven (Writer) and Cauron, Alfonso (director). *Harry Potter and the Prisoner of Azkaban.* Motuon picture. Warner Brothers. June 2004

Last Name Meanings. Online.www.last-names.net

London Underground. Online.tube.tfl.gov.uk

London Zoo. Online.www.londonzoo.co.uk

"Magikal Trees and Flowers," *Mystickblue.* Online.mystickblue.homestead.com/MagikalTreesandFlowers.html

Mangello, Louis A. *The Walt Disney World Trivia Book,* Intrepid Traveler. 2004.

"Mini," *GB Classic Cars.* Online.www.gbclassiccars.co.uk/mini.html

Mugglenet. Online.www.mugglenet.com

Mysterious Britain. Online.www.mysteriousbritain.co.uk

Mzimba, Lizo. "J.K. Rowling Talks about Book Four," *CBBC Newsround.* Online.news.bbc.co.uk/ccbcnews/. July 2000

"The origins of the Runes," *Oswald and the Runemaker.* Online.www.runemaker.com/hishome.htm

"Potts of Magic As Fan Buys Harry Book For 35,000," *Daily Record.* Online.www.dailyrecord.co.uk/. November 2003

Prisoner of Azkaban Movie News Site. Online.www.zanzaro.com/azkaban

Probert Encyclopedia of Mythology. Online.www.probertencyclopedia.com/mythology.htm

Raincoast Books. Online.www.raincoast.com/harrypotter/index.html

Rowling, J.K. (As Kenilworthy Whisp). *Quidditch through the Ages.* Vancouver: Raincoast Books, 2001

Rowling, J.K. (As Newt Scamader). *Fantastic Beasts & Where to Find Them.* Vancouver: Raincoast Books, 2001

Rowling, J.K. *AOL Chat.* Online. October 2001

Rowling, J.K. *Barnes & Noble Chat.* Online. October 2000

Rowling, J.K. *Comic Relief Chat.* Online.www.scholastic.com/harrypotter/author/transcipt3.htm. March 2001

Rowling, J.K. Harry Potter and Me. *BBC1 TV Special.* December 2001

Rowling, J.K. *Harry Potter and Philosopher's Stone*, Bloomsbury Press, 1997

Rowling, J.K. *Harry Potter and the Sorcerer's Stone*, Scholastic, Inc. 1997

Rowling, J.K. *Harry Potter and the Chamber of Secrets*, Scholastic, Inc. 1999

Rowling, J.K. *Harry Potter and the Prisoner of Azkaban*, Scholastic, Inc., 1999

Rowling, J.K. *Harry Potter and the Goblet of Fire*, Scholastic, Inc., 2000

Rowling, J.K. *Harry Potter and the Order of the Phoenix*, Scholastic, Inc., 2003

Rowling, J.K. *Interview with Evan Soloman on CBC.* July 2000

Rowling, J.K. *Interview with Jeremy Paxman on Newsnight.* June 2003.

Rowling, J.K. *Interview with Stephen Frye at Royal Albert Hall.* June 2003.

Rowling, J.K. Online. www.jkrowling.com

Rowling, J.K. *National Press Club* Interview.www.quick-quote-quill.org/articles/1999/1099-pressclubtransc.html. October 1999.

Rowling, J.K. *Scholastic.com Chat (number 1)* Online.Www.scholastic.com/harrypotter/author/transcipt1.htm.February 2000.

Rowling, J.K. *Scholastic.com Chat (number 2)* Online.Www.scholastic.com/harrypotter/author/transcipt2.htm. October 2000.

Rowling, J.K. *World Book Day Chat.* Online. March 2004

Rowling, J.K. *Yahooligans! Chat.* Online. Ocotber 2000

Scholastic Books. Online.www.scholastic.com/harrypotter

Sphinx's page. Online.www.nmia.com/-sphinx

The Leaky Cauldron. Online.www.the-leaky-cauldron.org

The Harry Potter Fan Zone.Omline.www.harrypotterfanzone.com

The Snitch. Online.www.thesnitch.co.uk

Tour UK. Online.www.touruk.co.uk

University of Oxford. Online.www.ox.ac.uk

What's In a Name? Online.www.theninemuses.net

Wizard News. Online.www.wizardnews.com

"XV World Cup USA '94," *World Cup History Page.* Online.www.worldcup.isn.pl/en/cups/1994.htm

ABOUT THE AUTHOR

Daniel Lawrence has been fascinated by Harry Potter (HP) since 1997, the first time he read *Harry Potter and the Philosopher's Stone* when it was initially published. At the time, a new wizard was just being introduced to the world. An expert and frequent speaker on the septology series, Lawrence is recognized by legions of Potter fans for his knowledge and authority in the many details that involve the beloved Harry Potter character. A valued contributor to Web sites and fan forums, he has read, examined and carefully dissected all the published books of J.K. Rowling and viewed all the films in the series hundreds of times. He has devoted a considerable amount of time and energy into learning everything he can about this "Magical World," amassing an extensive—and still growing—collection of Harry Potter memorabilia in the process. It includes books and articles about the six current books in the series and the four movies that have thus far been made. He has spent countless hours pouring over transcripts, diagrams, puzzles and information concerning the different worldwide versions of the septology.

About a year ago, while at an international group discussion, Lawrence was urged by those in attendance to "just do something" with all the plentiful knowledge he had accumulated in order to share more of Harry Potter's secrets, mysteries and facts with its millions of fans. The result is this book. He hopes it will increase your awareness and bring you additional magic whenever you read and discuss Harry Potter. Lawrence has a B.A degree from the University at Buffalo and a Doctorate from the University of Akron. His other interests include computers, travel, sports and personal fitness. Lawrence lives in Elma, New York, with his wife Lisa. He has three muggle children, including two daughters, Jenna and Sara, and a son Joey, who coincidentally was born on Harry Potter's birthday, July 31st.

Index

Italicized numbers reference subjects found in the answers sections of the book.

A

B

C

I

J

K

L

M

S

978-0-595-35500-6
0-595-35500-5